Helen Keller
Meet a Woman of Courage

Carin T. Ford

Enslow Publishers, Inc.

40 Industrial Road   PO Box 38
Box 398   Aldershot
Berkeley Heights, NJ 07922   Hants GU12 6BP
USA   UK

http://www.enslow.com

Library of Congress Cataloging-in-Publication Data

Ford, Carin T.
   Helen Keller : meet a woman of courage / Carin T. Ford.
      p. cm. — (Meeting famous people)
   Includes index.
   Summary: A biography of the deaf and blind woman who overcame her limitations to become a speaker, writer, and advocate for people with disabilities.
   ISBN 0-7660-1856-3 (hardcover)
   1. Keller, Helen, 1880–1968—Juvenile literature. 2. Blind—deaf women—United States—Biography—Juvenile literature. [1. Keller, Helen, 1880–1968. 2. Blind. 3. Deaf. 4. People with disabilities. 5. Women—Biography.] I. Title. II. Series.
   HV1624.K4 F673   2002
   362.4'1'092-dc21

                        2002000392

Printed in the United States of America

10 9 8 7 6 5 4 3 2 1

To Our Readers: We have done our best to make sure all Internet Addresses in this book were active and appropriate when we went to press. However, the author and the publisher have no control over and assume no liability for the material available on those Internet sites or on other Web sites they may link to. Any comments or suggestions can be sent by e-mail to comments@enslow.com or to the address on the back cover.

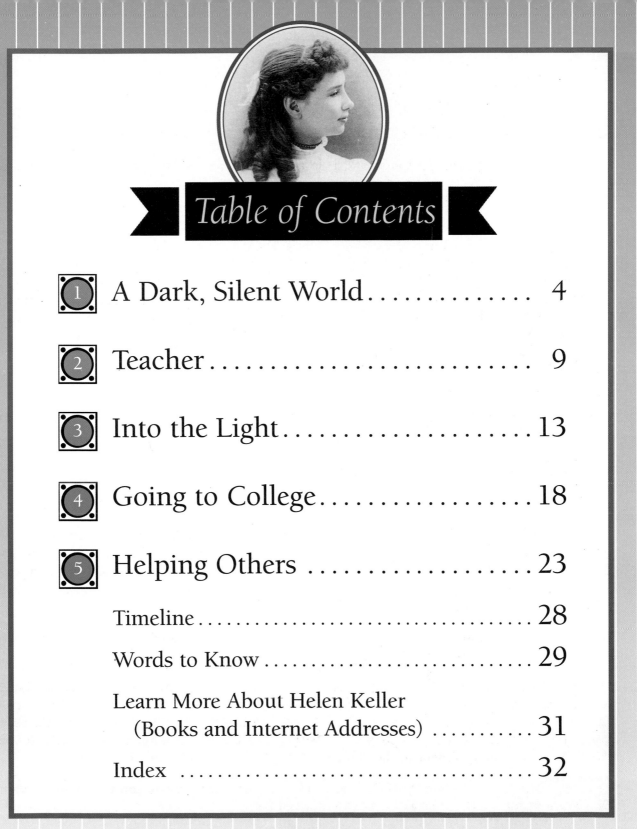

Table of Contents

Helen Keller, age seven, with her dog.

Chapter 1

A Dark, Silent World

Helen Keller was born on June 27, 1880, in Tuscumbia, Alabama. She was a happy little baby with blue eyes and curly hair.

She was smart, too. When she was only six months old, Helen could talk. She said "Howd'ye" for "how do you do," and "wah-wah" for "water." Her parents, Arthur and Kate, were proud of her.

When Helen was nineteen months old, she became

The Keller family home in Tuscumbia, Alabama. Helen was born in the small cottage at the right.

very sick. She had a high fever. The doctor did not know what was wrong with her. He thought Helen would die.

Helen was sick for a few days. When the fever left, her parents were very happy. But then they learned something terrible. Helen was now blind and deaf. Because she could not hear anything, soon she could not speak, either.

Helen knew she was not like everyone else. She touched people's mouths and felt them move their lips to talk. She did not know what it meant. This made her so angry that sometimes she would kick and scream.

She ran around the house smashing lamps and breaking dishes. During meals, Helen grabbed food off people's plates. She locked her mother in a closet. She pinched her grandmother. She even dumped her baby sister, Mildred, out of the cradle. Luckily, her mother caught the baby.

"I think I knew when I was naughty," Helen said. But she did not stop being bad.

Helen's parents felt very sorry for their daughter. So they did not punish her.

Helen could not see, hear,

Helen's parents, Kate and Arthur, worried about their little girl.

or speak. But she knew how to do many things. She could make ice cream and grind beans to make coffee. She could feed the hens in the yard. She even knew when visitors came to the house. She could smell them and feel their footsteps.

Helen's parents hoped she would be able to see and hear again one day. They took her to many doctors.

But no one could help her.

Helen knew that she was different.

Chapter 2

Teacher

he Kellers would not give up. They took a trip to Washington, D.C., to meet Alexander Graham Bell. He had invented the telephone. Bell also worked with deaf children. He taught them to speak.

Bell told the Kellers to write to the Perkins School for the Blind in Boston, Massachusetts. Maybe a teacher there could help Helen.

Bell was right. A woman named Anne Sullivan

traveled to Helen's home in 1887. Annie had never been a teacher before. She also had many problems with her eyes and could not see well. But she was excited about teaching Helen.

Annie tried to hug and kiss Helen when they first met. But Helen would not let her. Helen ran her fingers over Annie's face, dress, and bag. She tried to open the bag, but her mother took it away. Helen kicked and screamed. Annie put Helen's hand on her watch. She showed Helen how to open it. Helen liked the watch, and she stopped screaming.

But not for long.

Helen and Annie had many fights. Helen pinched Annie. She even knocked out one of Annie's front teeth!

At meals, Annie would not let Helen grab food off people's plates. She made Helen sit in her chair and eat with a spoon.

Annie Sullivan became Helen's teacher.

Soon Helen learned to behave. Annie taught her to sew. She also spelled words into Helen's hand with her fingers. Helen knew the finger spellings for many words, like doll, hat, and cake. But it was a game to Helen. She did not really know what the words meant.

One day, when Helen was almost seven, Annie took Helen outside to the water pump at the well. Annie spelled w-a-t-e-r as the water spilled onto Helen's hand. And suddenly, Helen understood.

"I knew then that 'w-a-t-e-r' meant the wonderful cool something that was flowing over my hand," she said.

Helen fell to the ground and pointed. What was its name? She patted the water pump. What was its name?

Then Helen pointed to Annie. What was *her* name? Annie spelled into Helen's hand, "T-e-a-c-h-e-r." Annie Sullivan was Teacher. And that is what Helen would always call her.

Annie, right, taught Helen how to "talk" to the rest of the world.

Chapter 3

Into the Light

As soon as Helen woke up in the morning, she wanted to spell with her fingers. When Annie was not talking to her, Helen spelled into her *own* hand—she was talking to herself!

She learned about the world through her fingers. She took walks with Annie and felt flowers, butterflies, and small animals. Helen felt a baby chick pecking its way out of a shell. At the circus, she rode an elephant, hugged a young lion, and shook hands with a bear.

Helen visited the Perkins School for the Blind, right. The director, Michael Anagnos, below, thought she was very smart.

Helen learned how to read, too. She had books with raised letters. She felt the shapes of the letters with her fingertips.

Helen was taught to write in square-hand. The letters had only straight lines, no curves. When Helen was seven, she wrote her mother a letter:

"Helen will write mother letter . . . papa did give helen drink of water . . . helen will hug and kiss mother . . . mother does love helen."

Annie also taught Helen how to read and write Braille. The Braille alphabet is made up of raised dots that blind people feel with their fingertips.

Christmas that year was special for the Kellers. They were very glad that Annie had come to teach Helen. Now Helen was happy and polite. She could talk to her family with her fingers.

But there was still one thing Helen wanted to do. She wanted to speak. Helen traveled to Boston to study with a special teacher. She put her fingers on the teacher's lips and tongue when she spoke. Then Helen tried to move her own lips and tongue

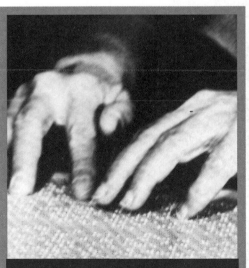

Helen learned to read with her fingertips.

the same way. "It is warm," Helen said after much practice. It was her first sentence.

When Helen was fourteen, she attended a school for the deaf in New York City. Helen hoped she would learn how to speak more clearly.

Helen studied hard. She also played checkers, learned how to ride a horse, and had a part in the school play. A student at the school said Helen could read the writing on blackboards. She used her fingers to trace the chalk marks.

Helen enjoyed school and she still wanted to learn many things. She decided to do something no blind and deaf person had done before. She decided to go to college.

Helen could feel words on the blackboard. She read the chalk marks with her fingers.

Helen, left, and Annie, center, met many famous
people, such as the inventor Alexander Graham Bell.

Chapter 4

Going to College

adcliffe College did not want Helen. People at the school thought the work would be too hard for a woman who could not see or hear. Some of Helen's friends agreed.

But Helen had always been a fighter. She set out to prove everyone wrong.

The work *was* hard. Annie sat by Helen in class, spelling everything the teacher said into her hand.

Math was very hard for Helen. Making shapes with wires helped her learn about triangles and circles.

After class, Helen would hurry home. She used her Braille typewriter to write down everything she could remember from class.

Helen had fun in college. She swam, played chess and checkers, and rode a two-seater bicycle. She was even voted vice president of her class.

But sometimes Helen was sad and lonely. She knew she was not like the other students. Most students could not spell with their fingers. So they could not "talk" to Helen. Still, everyone liked Helen. They gave her a gift—a dog she named Phiz.

While in college, Helen was asked to write a story about her life for a magazine called *Ladies' Home Journal*. The magazine would pay her $3,000 to tell about her life. Helen was excited. But she had a lot of schoolwork and Annie's eyes

Annie, right, sat next to Helen in every class and told her what the teachers said.

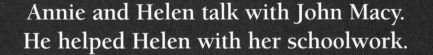
Annie and Helen talk with John Macy.
He helped Helen with her schoolwork.

were hurting her. Helen could not do it alone. John Macy, an English teacher at Harvard College, said he would help.

The magazine story became a book, called *The Story of My Life*. John Macy stayed and helped Helen with her college work. Helen graduated with honors in 1904. The next year, John and Annie got married.

Helen kept writing. She also traveled and spoke to many people. She wanted everyone to learn about blindness and how to prevent it.

Helen wanted to speak clearly and look her best when she talked to people. She practiced speaking. She also went to a doctor and had an operation on her eyes. Ever since she went blind, Helen's left eye jutted out. Now she had her eyes removed and replaced with glass ones that looked better.

Helen had strong feelings about many things. Before 1920, women did not have the right to vote. Helen believed this was wrong. She marched in parades with other women who felt the same way.

Helen did not like it when people only asked to hear about her life. She enjoyed talking about ideas and what was going on in the world, too. Helen wanted people to know she had a mind of her own.

Chapter 5

Helping Others

As the years went on, Annie felt ill and tired much of the time. Her eyesight was so bad, she was nearly blind.

A woman named Polly Thomson came to help Helen and Annie. She became the ears for Helen and the eyes for both Helen and Annie.

A man named Peter Fagan also began working for Helen. He learned how to read Braille and how to spell with his fingers. Peter fell in love with Helen. He asked her to marry him, and Helen said yes. But Helen's mother did not think this was a good idea. She would not let Helen visit with Peter anymore.

At this time, Helen traveled to Hollywood, California. She was going to be in the movies.

The movie was called *Deliverance* and told the story of Helen's life. Annie was in it, too. Polly spelled into Helen's hand what she was supposed to do—walk over to a window, act surprised, hold up her hands to the sun.

Helen also performed in the theater. She and Annie stood on stage for twenty minutes. They told the story of how Helen had learned the meaning of words. The audience asked Helen many questions: "Do you close

> **Helen was famous. Everyone wanted to know about her.**

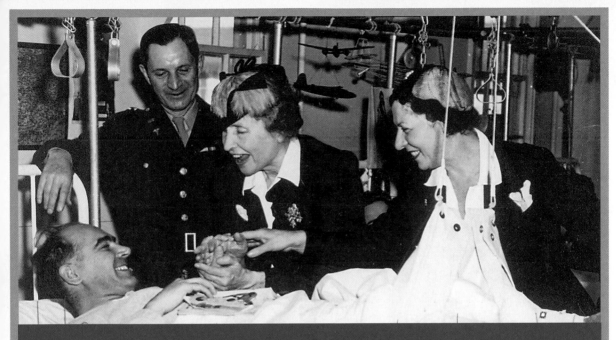

Helen and Polly, right, visited many hospitals.
They talked to soldiers about hope and courage.

your eyes when you sleep?" "Can you tell the time of day without a watch?" "What is your idea of color?"

Helen and Annie traveled to many different places raising money for the blind. Helen also helped set up libraries for blind people all over the country.

Annie died at the age of seventy with Helen holding her hand. Helen was so sad.

Polly stayed with Helen. They traveled all over the world. During World War II, Helen visited many hospitals. She talked to soldiers who were hurt. Many of them were blind and deaf like Helen. She told them never to give up.

Polly died in 1960. Helen was eighty years old and was known as the greatest woman alive in the United States. She was awarded the Presidential Medal of Freedom in 1964. She was also elected to the Women's Hall of Fame.

Helen would always remember Annie, her first teacher.

Helen died on June 1, 1968. She had been blind and deaf since she was a baby. But that did not stop Helen from doing all the things she wanted to do. She was a brave woman who spent her life helping other people.

Helen Keller did more than anyone
had thought possible.

Timeline

1880~Born in Tuscumbia, Alabama, on June 27.

1887~Annie Sullivan becomes Helen's teacher. Helen learns that words have meanings.

1890~Begins voice lessons to learn to speak.

1903~Publishes *The Story of My Life*.

1904~Graduates from Radcliffe College.

1919~Appears in *Deliverance*, a movie about her life.

1924~Begins raising money for the American Foundation for the Blind.

1931~Helps create a national system of libraries for the blind.

1943~Begins her visits to injured soldiers in hospitals.

1964~Helen is awarded the Presidential Medal of Freedom.

1968~Dies on June 1.

Braille—A system of printing for blind people. Raised dots stand for the letters of the alphabet. People "read" words by touching the dots with their fingertips.

Braille typewriter—a keyboard for typing Braille.

Presidential Medal of Freedom—A medal given by the president of the United States. It is the highest award given to a citizen of this nation.

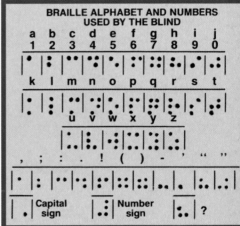

Radcliffe College—a famous school linked with Harvard College in Cambridge, Massachusetts. It used to be for women only.

This is the Braille alphabet. (The dots have been colored black so they show in this picture.)

water pump—a device that draws water up from deep in the ground.

Women's Hall of Fame—A national museum honoring important American women. It is located in Seneca Falls, New York.

World War II—A war that was fought in Europe, North Africa, and Asia from 1939 to 1945.

"*W-a-t-e-r.*"
Helen learned the meaning of words at this water pump.

Learn More

Books

Adler, David A. *A Picture Book of Helen Keller*.
New York: Holiday House, 1990.

Baker, Pamela J. *My First Book of Sign*.
Lake Forest, Ill.: Forest House, 1992.

Hurwitz, Johanna. *Helen Keller: Courage in the Dark*.
New York: Random House, 1997.

Internet Addresses

American Federation for the Blind:
Helen Keller photos, letters, speeches.
<http://www.afb.org/info_documents.asp?
collectionid=1>

Perkins School for the Blind's Helen Keller page.
<http://www.perkins.pvt.k12.ma.us/area.php?id=3>

Index

JB KELLER F
Ford, Carin T.
Helen Keller

$17.95